DODD, MEAD WONDERS BOOKS

Wonders of the Mosquito World by Phil Ault
Wonders of the World of Bears by Bernadine Bailey
Wonders of Animal Migration by Jacquelyn Berrill
Wonders of Animal Nurseries by Jacquelyn Berrill
Wonders of the Arctic by Jacquelyn Berrill
Wonders of the Monkey World by Jacquelyn Berrill
Wonders of the Woods and Desert at Night by Jacquelyn Berrill
Wonders of the World of Wolves by Jacquelyn Berrill
Wonders of Alligators and Crocodiles by Wyatt Blassingame
Wonders of Frogs and Toads by Wyatt Blassingame
Wonders of a Kelp Forest by Joseph E. Brown
Wonders of Rattlesnakes by G. Earl Chace
Wonders of the Pelican World by Joseph J. Cook and Ralph W. Schreiber
Wonders Inside You by Margaret Cosgrove
Wonders of the Tree World by Margaret Cosgrove
Wonders of Your Senses by Margaret Cosgrove
Wonders of Wild Ducks by Thomas D. Fegely
Wonders Beyond the Solar System by Rocco Feravolo
Wonders of Gravity by Rocco Feravolo
Wonders of Mathematics by Rocco Feravolo
Wonders of Sound by Rocco Feravolo
Wonders of the World of the Albatross by Harvey I. and Mildred L. Fisher
Wonders of the World of Shells by Morris K. Jacobson and William K. Emerson
Wonders of Animal Architecture by Sigmund A. Lavine
Wonders of the Bat World by Sigmund A. Lavine
Wonders of the Cactus World by Sigmund A. Lavine
Wonders of the Eagle World by Sigmund A. Lavine
Wonders of the Fly World by Sigmund A. Lavine
Wonders of the Hawk World by Sigmund A. Lavine
Wonders of the Owl World by Sigmund A. Lavine
Wonders of the Spider World by Sigmund A. Lavine
Wonders of the World of Horses by Sigmund A. Lavine and Brigid Casey
Wonders of the Bison World by Sigmund A. Lavine and Vincent Scuro
Wonders of Magnets and Magnetism by Owen S. Lieberg
Wonders of Measurement by Owen S. Lieberg
Wonders of the Dinosaur World by William H. Matthews III
Wonders of Fossils by William H. Matthews III
Wonders of Sand by Christie McFall
Wonders of Stones by Christie McFall
Wonders of Gems by Richard M. Pearl
Wonders of Rocks and Minerals by Richard M. Pearl
Wonders of Barnacles by Arnold Ross and William K. Emerson
Wonders of Seagulls by Elizabeth and Ralph Schreiber
Wonders of Hummingbirds by Hilda Simon

WONDERS OF RATTLESNAKES

G. Earl Chace
Illustrated with photographs by the author

598.1
C
8240

DODD, MEAD & COMPANY · NEW YORK

Frontispiece: An adult, alert prairie rattlesnake, *Crotalus v. viridis*

ACKNOWLEDGMENTS

Although I have practically lived with, caught, studied, and cared for rattlesnakes for four or more decades, I could never have put their story into acceptable words without the able assistance of two sympathetic ladies. First, my wife, Edith, who not only retyped my manuscript but corrected my many mistakes, and secondly, editor Jennifer Anderson, who somehow steered my many thoughts and words into an acceptable form for publication.

The photograph on page 15, courtesy of Jack Tscharner

Library of Congress Cataloging in Publication Data

Chace, G   Earl.
    Wonders of rattlesnakes.

    SUMMARY: Introduces the physical characteristics, habits, and environment of various kinds of rattlesnakes with emphasis on the prairie rattler. Also discusses myths about this reptile and precautions to take in rattlesnake country.
    1. Rattlesnakes—Juvenile literature. [1. Rattlesnakes. 2. Snakes] I. Title.
QL666.069C48   598.1′2   75-11430
ISBN 0-396-07176-7

To two small, wonderful granddaughters, C. Brook Chace and Jessica Parker. May they grow up to love and respect nature as I have always done.

Contents

The western diamondback, *Crotalus atrox*, is identified by the row of brownish diamonds on a grayish background, and by the black and white bands on its tail.

CHAPTER 1
Introducing the Rattlesnake

Rattlesnakes are reptiles and belong to a family called the pit vipers or Crotalidae. All pit vipers have long, curved fangs attached to the front of the upper jaw; they can be folded back to lie out of sight inside the mouth or extended out beyond the snake's nose when it intends to bite. They also have two heat sensitive organs recessed in pits located behind and below each nostril, are poisonous, and, like all snakes, are deaf. The only characteristic separating the rattlesnake from all other pit vipers, therefore, is the rattle on its tail.

Rattlesnakes are rough-scaled, heavy-bodied snakes that are considered to be highly dangerous. They are dangerous because they are poisonous, have hair-trigger temperaments, and can strike up to their full length with considerable speed and accuracy. Some people seem unable to tell them from other types of snakes, but all wear the brown, loosely attached rattle on the end of their tail. They wear it from birth to death, and no other type of snake in the world has anything like it. Rattlesnakes are considered by many scientists to be the highest evolved of the snakes. The complicated, hollow, movable fangs place the pit vipers high on the evolutionary scale, but the addition of a rattle places the rattlers above this.

9

Evolved from the amphibian during the Carboniferous period about 300 million years ago, reptiles prospered into infinite varieties and immense sizes. They completely dominated the world for millions of years and then, for little known reasons, began to decline. About 100 million years ago and during the demise of the giant reptiles, or dinosaurs, the snake began to make its appearance. It evolved from at least one species of small lizard, and the first snake fossil remains are mingled with those of the last dinosaurs.

Anatomically, snakes and lizards have a lot in common. In fact, together they form the order Squamata, and the presence or absence of legs is not the differentiating characteristic. Some boa constrictors and pythons still have vestigial legs, and there is at least one type of legless lizard named *Ophisaurus*. The change from lizard to snake did cost the snake the loss of movable eyelids, the ability to hear airborne sounds, and a solid chin, all of which are still found in lizards and form the three major differences between lizards and snakes.

The fossil record of snakes is not too clear. Neither skin nor rattles readily fossilize, and the small, delicate bone structures tend to become scattered and practically unreadable. Enough have been found, however, to show that the first rattlesnake made its appearance somewhere between 4 and 12 million years ago.

There are many types of rattlesnakes. Herpetologists, or reptile-amphibian scientists, have divided them into about 30 species and 65 subspecies, and they are all found in either North, Central, or South America. They were discovered when the first Europeans came to the New World sometime in the fifteenth century. The early Spanish-speaking explorers called them the Cascabel, which translates roughly into "little bell" and undoubtedly refers to the rattle. Knowing only the one small poisonous snake in Europe, the explorers were not pre-

The black-tailed rattlesnake, *Crotalus m. molossus*, was named for its black tail, but it also has a dark blotch over the nose and dark markings that contrast with its yellowish or greenish background.

pared for the great size, noisiness, and potential of the American rattlesnakes and wrote reports full of exaggerated, untrue, or imaginative tales which some people still believe.

Rattlesnakes come in all sizes, from those only 18 inches long when full grown to some species which reach almost 8 feet in length. They were once found in considerable numbers throughout their range, but as people move in to farm the land, build their cities and towns and construct their highways, they

11

either destroy the small mammals which make up the food of the snake, or kill the snakes themselves. Not only is the quantity of snakes diminishing, but also the size. The larger snakes are more readily seen and exterminated, and the younger ones seldom have the chance to grow to full size.

Rattlesnakes are not particularly long-lived, at least not in zoos, and records made in confinement are the only ones possible to obtain. Rattlers give birth to living young, and, although many have been born and raised in captivity, public objections overrule any suggestions concerning marking and releasing young poisonous snakes as scientists do with banded birds. Life expectancy of snakes seems to vary with the size they attain, and only a few large species have lived ten years or more in cages. The record is fourteen years. However, because rattlesnakes are an extremely nervous breed, there is little doubt that a longer life can be expected of the free snake.

Many people fear the rattlesnake because they have heard that it will chase them, jump through the air, and strike for no apparent reason. Most snake men agree that the strike of a rattler is more defensive than offensive. During the Revolutionary War, men of Virginia and South Carolina who lived in rattlesnake territory and knew the rattlesnake, devised a flag consisting of the picture of a coiled rattler ready to strike and the simple caption, "Don't Tread on Me." Its meaning was clear; neither the men nor the snake desired to fight, but if pushed, would do so.

The United States is divided into various biological areas called biomes. Each biome has a specific climate, soil, terrain, and altitude, plus all the plants, trees, and creatures that do best under such conditions. There are twenty-six species of rattlesnake in this country, and each species prefers a particular type of biome, and stays there. The large timber rattler (*Crotalus h. horridus*) of the eastern United States is dependent upon the

12

The timber rattler, *Crotalus h. horridus*, has two color phases. Some have yellow background with brown bands, and others are brown with black bands. Often called banded rattlers, or, if very dark, velvet tails.

deciduous forests of that region. It also needs the rocky out-croppings that pop up all through this area like little islands in a sea. A colony, or den, of snakes on one such island rarely prowls for more than a few miles from its ancestral home and must return before winter sets in.

The low, wet, hummock country of the southeastern states is home to the huge eastern diamondback (*Crotalus adamanteus*). Known to reach almost 8 feet in length and a weight of about 20 pounds, this snake is considered to be among the most danger-ous snakes of the world.

The eastern diamondback rattlesnake, *Crotalus adamanteus*, is much darker than its western cousin, lacks the vivid tail bands, and is larger.

The western diamondback (*Crotalus atrox*) is probably the best known, most publicized, and most feared rattler in the United States. Second only to the eastern diamondback rattler in size, it dwells throughout much of the arid southwest and has the most explosive disposition of all rattlers. It was once found in unprecedented numbers, but civilization and thrill collectors are slowly but surely diminishing its numbers. In one spring hunt of 1961, thrill collectors delivered 13,976 pounds of live western diamondbacks to a South Dakota reptile exhibit.

The hot, dry deserts of the Southwest, where the sands are loose and the surface is cactus studded, are the domain of the little sidewinder rattlesnake (*Crotalus cerastes*). He gained the name by developing a strange but effective sideways, loping

14

The author counted and checked in nearly seven tons of western diamond-backs at the Black Hills Reptile Gardens in 1961.

movement that enables him to traverse such loose, sandy areas with ease. He is also called the horned rattler because of two elongated scales that stand up over his eyes.

Another timber rattler, also called the Pacific rattler (*Crotalus oreganus*), inhabits the pine and spruce forested areas of the western United States and, like its eastern cousin, also frequents the rock islands amidst the trees.

In between these biomes is the high prairie that reaches all through the center of the country and is home to the prairie rattler (*Crotalus v. viridis*), which is to be the prime concern of this book. All rattlesnakes are primarily alike, differing mainly in size, coloration, and the area in which they are found, but the prairie rattlesnake is truly an unusual snake. It has the

The sidewinder, *Crotalus cerastes*, can readily be identified by the horn-like scales over its eyes. It can either be light brown or gray in color, with darker brown blotches on its back.

ability to live and thrive on the high prairie biome which is one of the most inhospitable habitats of all.

All of the rattlesnakes thus far mentioned belong to the genus *Crotalus* because they have many small scales covering the top of their head. Members of another genus, *Sistrurus*, have but nine

A cluster of small scales covering the nose and extending between the eyes is indicative of the genus *Crotalus*.

A few, usually nine, large scales cover the nose and the area between the eyes of the massasauga, *Sistrurus catenatus tergeminus*, and snakes of the entire genus *Sistrurus*. Dark blotches on a tan background mark this "swamp rattler."

large scales covering their head. Called ground or pygmy rattlers, these are usually quite small with a corresponding tiny rattle that is both difficult to see or hear. One type, called the massasauga (*Sistrurus catenatus*) haunts swampy areas and eats frogs. The ground or pygmy rattlers (*Sistrurus miliarius*) seldom grow beyond 18 inches long and live in the woodlands. They inhabit the eastern half of the United States.

Rattlesnakes, like all reptiles, are cold-blooded or ectothermic. They have little or no body heat of their own, so must gain warmth from the surrounding air. The cold winters of North America force the rattlers to hibernate deep in the ground where the frost will not kill them. This is one reason why North American rattlers seldom travel far from adequate dens. In South and Central America, a never-freezing climate allows the snakes to roam more freely, and the specimens are more widely scattered. The rattlers of these regions are almost all of the larger diamondback types with difficult scientific names such as *Crotalus durissus terrificus*. These are the snakes named Cascabel by the Spanish people whose fears were justified when science found the tropical rattlesnakes to have a consistently more deadly and faster-acting venom than the North American varieties.

These are the main and better known species of rattlesnakes. Scattered through the same biomes, or gathered in smaller isolated biomes, are the lesser species and subspecies of rattlers. So well do these biological boundaries work that quick identification of a species of rattler is often made by the area in which it is found, rather than the longer, but more scientific method of counting almost each and every scale on the snake's body and checking for the presence or absence of specific scales. A snake's scalation is quite consistent within a species, and the scale count is almost as accurate an identification of a species of snake as fingerprints are of a human individual.

CHAPTER 2

The Prairie Rattlesnake

The high prairie country is a great expanse of short grass that extends from Canada to Mexico. It begins at the foothills of the Rocky Mountains and stretches for several hundred miles eastward. At its eastern edge it is about 2,000 feet above sea level and from here rises to about 6,000 feet at the edge of the mountains.

That the prairie rattlesnake can live here at all is remarkable. Being cold-blooded or ectothermic, the snake finds it difficult to move or even digest its meals when the weather grows too cold, or below 45 degrees Fahrenheit, and is likely to die when it grows too warm, or above 95 degrees. It prefers a temperature of between 75 and 85 degrees. The snake has to keep on the move, searching for shaded areas when too warm or seeking sunny spots when it becomes too cold. All rattlesnakes must do this, but the fluctuations and extremes of this great biome are exceptional.

There are no large bodies of water on the high prairie to absorb the summer's excessive heat and release it again when winter comes. Neither does the thin, dry air buffer fast temperature changes as the heavier, more sultry air does for the lower lands. There can be a rise or fall of 50 degrees in a single day

19

Under the shadows of the Rocky Mountains lies the high western edge of prairie rattler domain.

and as much of a seasonal change as 140 degrees, from 115 in the summer to 25 degrees below zero in the winter.

Before man invaded and utilized the prairie for his own, there were millions upon millions of prairie dogs scattered all over. The dog towns covered thousands of square miles and their holes were everywhere. The prairie rattler was then in its heyday; it ate young dogs and was never too far from a hole into which it could crawl whenever danger threatened, be it animal or weather. When man came and began to plant his crops and raise his cattle, he could not successfully compete with the appetites of the prairie dogs which ate the same crops and grasses that fed both man and cattle, so he poisoned them wholesale. Today, the rattler has to utilize the fractured rock bases of the

20

buttes and mesas for shelter and depend upon the smaller rodents for food.

When the prairie dogs and their holes pockmarked the land, the snake could range far and wide, yet always find a lifesaving burrow nearby. Without them, rattlesnakes must limit their seasonal travels to about three miles from their dens. These holes are important to the snake because it has no sweat glands. When mammals, which have such glands, grow too warm, they automatically begin to sweat, and the issuing moisture brings some of the excessive body heat out with it. Passing breezes evaporate this moisture, and the process tends to cool the mammal more. The rattler, lacking these glands, continues to grow hotter and hotter and unless it can reach a cool place it will die. Biologists have learned that when the temperature at the height of a man standing on the prairie reaches 90 degrees Fahrenheit, the snake on the ground may be subjected to 119 degrees, but a short way down a hole, the temperature will be only 80 degrees. Spring storms can suddenly reduce the temperature to 20 de-

The young of these prairie dogs may serve as food for hungry rattlers.

grees, but down in the hole the soil will keep the air temperature at about 40 degrees.

Some species of rattlesnake may be facing extinction because of encroaching civilization, but the prairie rattler, due to its vast, lightly populated biome should last indefinitely. Although hunted near human habitats, there are still great areas where this rattler can live much as it always has. The high plains, because of the inclement weather, short growing season, alkaline soils, and little rainfall proved to be of little value to the vegetable farmer, so much of the land is used for grazing. Beef cattle need a lot of food and it takes anywhere up to forty acres to supply enough grazing for one animal during a dry season. Cattle ranches are therefore huge; sizable cities are several hundreds of miles apart; towns are small, with close to a hundred miles separating many of them; even the ranch houses are seldom within sight of one another. The land is crisscrossed with barbwire fences which offer no obstacle to a snake, and, except for the lack of the prairie dog towns, the biome is much as it always has been. Many of the prairie snakes undoubtedly live a full life and never see a human.

The prairie rattler is not a large snake. The northern snakes average about 3 feet long and seldom much over 2 pounds in weight. In the south, due to warmer weather and a resulting longer feeding season, they grow larger, with a maximum recorded length of 5 feet. Their bodies are colored gray-green and are marked with darker brownish blotches that closely resemble the shaded portions of a leaf or clump of grass. Such colors provide the snake with excellent camouflage among the prairie plants.

The prairie biome offers only four months of feeding weather. It is almost June before the prairie rattlers can come out of their dens and begin to hunt, and by mid-September the cold north winds begin to blow, and the rattlers must again seek

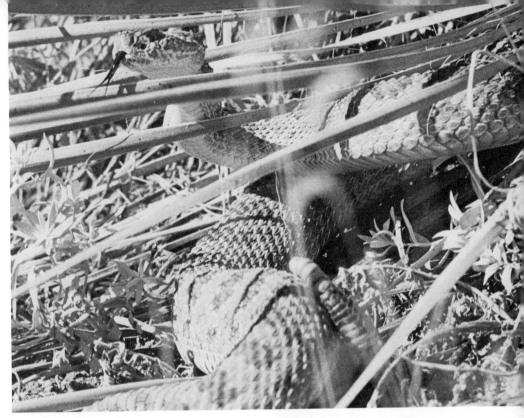

A yucca plant provides both shade from a broiling sun and camouflage from possible enemies.

hibernation quarters, or freeze. In between these periods of hibernation, the prairie often becomes too hot for the snakes to hunt their prey during the day, so, like the desert rattlers, they hide from the sun and do much of their hunting at night.

The nature of these plains offers hazards that most other rattlers seldom encounter. The great, predominantly treeless area presents little in the way of protective cover. Snakes of the forests can hide in the underbrush. Snakes of rocky areas can crawl into any of the cactus patches. The prairie rattler must spend much of its time on the wide open spaces made of hard-packed soil which it cannot penetrate by itself, and with only short grass to screen its movements. It is also, like all snakes, deaf and incapable of hearing the approach of an enemy, the rustle of

23

The snake checks the air with its tongue in an effort to discover what may be approaching.

a mouse for food, or the winds that signal a potential hail storm. Finally, snakes are not noted for being highly intelligent, so must rely on instinct. With the exception of mating, adult and newborn snakes react the same way for the same reasons.

Snakes do have individual characteristics. Some take longer to act at all in any given situation, and others overreact. I have seen, walked up to, and captured rattlesnakes that were no more trouble than picking up a plastic snake, while others were like a fused bomb that exploded when I reached them. Because of these differences, there is always excitement when approaching a wild rattlesnake. Once your approach is suspected, the snake

24

raises its head to see you, but long before you come into its visual range, the snake begins to flick its tongue in an effort to identify you by odor. Some snakes, assured of their camouflage, may lie quietly and allow you to pass by, while others make some effort to retreat. Most of them, as you get closer and closer, manifest their nervousness by starting their well-known buzzing.

The snake that really thrills, frightens, or awes the human interloper is the one that decides to make a fight of it. Snapping to the alert, it loosens its coils so that its entire forebody is free

Although this is the exaggerated striking position of a prairie rattlesnake, occasionally it is one of a frightened snake. Note that although at full alert, the snake is not rattling.

of entanglements. This portion of the body is then elevated and drawn back into a wide curve to provide it with the maximum thrust. Its body flattens and its belly widens to give it more traction on the ground. The tongue, rather than flicking, sticks out and bends both up and down, but is held for long moments in either direction. The end of its tail becomes a blur and the sound of its rattle is continuous. The entire snake is plainly declaring war.

War to such a snake is the strike. Seldom does a snake move closer to a person to get a better chance. If you walk away from this cold-blooded warrior, he waits until it is certain that you have left, then slowly leaves. If you continue to approach, the snake strikes. The strike is normally made once only, but on occasions, really nasty individuals continue to strike repeatedly, but only for a short time. Mouth open, it starts its strike and the

The scent of man sends this snake back into its den for protection.

fangs are erected. At the end of the strike the body is recoiled, the fangs retracted, and the mouth closed. Only in rare cases does a snake strike more than its full length. The usual strike is one-third or one-half of the snake's full length. Too long a reach throws the snake completely off balance and at the mercy of its enemy.

Most rattlesnakes do not continue striking because they have little endurance. Unlike the mammal or bird which has a 4-chambered heart and two efficient lungs, the rattler has a 3-chambered heart which provides a poor circulatory system and one good lung that brings in too little oxygen for anything but short bursts of action. Great or prolonged activity burns up stored energy faster than it can be replaced, so snakes are forced to stop and rest frequently. Except for eating, evading enemies, or mating, the rattlers lead a slow, restful, placid life.

CHAPTER 3

Physical Characteristics

In the course of the snake's evolution, certain of its organs have been changed or modified. Some organs, such as the 3-valved heart are merely evolutionary stepping-stones to the modern-day, 4-valved heart of mammals. Other features, such as the rattlesnake's heat sensory pits, seem to be unique to certain snakes, and have evolved no further.

Internally, the snake is supported by numerous vertebrae and ribs, the numbers varying with the species, but no long or heavy bones. It is well muscled. The circulatory system is poor, having the 3-valved heart and no complete removal of waste products in the blood or efficient reoxygenation such as mammals have. Good and bad blood are freely mixed. Respiration is also poor; one lung is usually degenerate, and although the functioning lung is long (frequently over half the length of the snake), a large portion acts merely as an air reservoir and exchanges no gasses with the blood. When inflated, it does act as an excellent swim bladder and easily supports a swimming snake. The trachea can extend out of the snake's mouth and suck air when a large animal that is being swallowed blocks the mouth and throat for a long period.

The throat, esophagus, and stomach all have longitudinal

folds that allow these organs to stretch and accommodate large food animals. The intestine leads to the vent or cloaca of the snake which is located on the underside of the body where the tail begins. It is the only opening on the snake other than those of the head, and is used for all three functions—elimination, mating, and birth. The sexes are separate, although there is no readily apparent external difference between them.

Snakes do have some portions of an internal ear and seem capable of hearing heavy sound waves, such as thunder, but otherwise they are deaf to the air waves that mammals and birds

Variations in the prairie rattler with altered markings, red tongue, and speckled scales. Such misfits are occasionally found in any species of snake.

construe as sounds. The few sounds that are received by the snake's ears are transmitted to its jawbones and merely register as a series of vibrations. Snakes are, however, quite aware of any vibrations in the ground they lie upon.

Snake Skin Is Different

Both snakes and fish wear scales all over their bodies for protection. There is, however, considerable difference in these scales. Fish scales are attached to the skin, whereas the scales of the snake are the skin. One scale can easily be plucked from the side of a fish but not from a snake. Should one snake scale be pulled hard enough, an entire section of the skin would be torn off. The skin of a snake is folded over and over in intricate patterns, and the small, individual layers we call scales have been thickened and hardened into an effective armor. The thin skin between each scale is capable of considerable stretching and allows the snake maneuverability. Some snake scales are smooth, and the body looks wet or shiny and is therefore often called "slimy," though both skin and scales are perfectly dry. The scales of the rattlesnake are rough or keeled, with each scale having a thin, hard ridge running through its center much like the midrib of a leaf.

The belly scales of the rattlesnake are necessary to its locomotion. These are also continuous with the skin, but are short and wide, extending all the way across the snake's belly. They overlap one another like the clapboards on the side of a house. The loose edges are toward the snake's tail. These scales are always smooth and shiny to allow easy forward movement by the snake, but the loose, rear edges catch on any irregularity of the ground and prevent the snake from slipping backward.

Scales offer protection to the snakes as they crawl among the rocks and brush. Desert rattlers have been seen climbing up the sides of cacti that were covered with sharp spines, paying no

The head of the Mexican west coast rattlesnake, *Crotalus b. basiliscus*. Due to its diamond markings and green coloration, it is also called the Mexican green diamondback.

attention to them. Occasionally, captured rattlers are found with cactus needles stuck between their scales, but usually only around the head area. This is presumably a result of the snake striking at prey hiding in a cactus patch.

Snake skin wears out and must be replaced. In fact, the skin of all large creatures is eventually replaced. Mammal skin is shed gradually by flaking and is replaced the same way, one bit at a time. Snakes shed their skin all at once and in one large piece. Under the shed skin is a new, immaculate, larger skin, fitted and ready for wear.

The prairie rattler sheds on an average of three times each summer. The portion of skin that is shed is called the epidermal layer and is the thin, transparent outer layer of the entire skin.

Rattlesnake skin is tough and waterproof.

The snake begins by rubbing its nose on the ground until the skin is pushed up over the nose and loosened from the lower jaws. Then, by rippling its body muscles and at the same time crawling through grass, weeds, and rocks that tend to hold back the shedding skin, the snake crawls right through the mouth opening in the skin and leaves it behind as one long, inside out, colorless tube. On the body of the snake, this skin is folded under, around, and over every scale. When shed, the skin is flattened and stretched until it is much larger around and several inches longer than the snake that left it.

The faster a snake grows, the more frequently it sheds—and the more food it eats, the faster it grows. During a long, warm summer, the rattler may find and eat many mice and be forced to shed four or more times. In a short, cold summer, the snake will be so inactive due to this cold that it barely eats enough to

32

stay alive and may shed only once or twice.

Herpetologists use snake scales for more or less positive identification of each species. Each scale on a snake's body has an assigned name and number. There are about 2,700 species of snakes in the world and an enormous number of scales on each snake. This, plus the fact that minute variations of arrangement are found within each species, creates disagreements among the taxonomists who identify and name snakes. They argue over whether a certain snake is different enough to be a species, a subspecies, or a variety. It is for this reason that the word "about" is used when quoting figures on the number of species of snakes there are.

The Eyes

The rattlesnake has good eyes but for close vision only, sight being limited to about 12 or 15 feet. The pupils of its eyes change shape as the light grows brighter or dimmer, much as the diaphragm of a camera is changed when taking pictures in dif-

In bright daylight, the pupils of a rattlesnake's eyes are narrow, vertical slits.

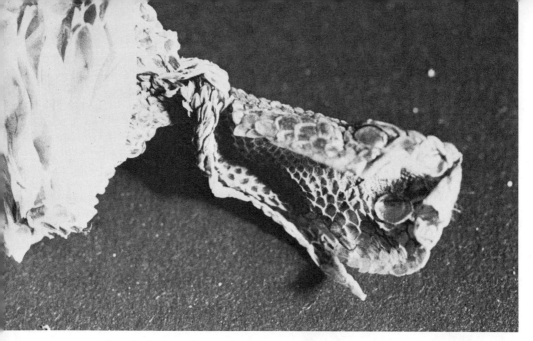

The shed skin of a rattlesnake retains the outer layer of the eye shields. The upper shield shows the outer view, and the lower shield shows the view from the inside of the shed skin.

ferent light. During the bright day, its pupils are narrow, vertical slits that extend over the full diameter of the eye, but when it hunts by night, as it often does, the pupils become large and round, allowing more light to pass inside. The eyes have no movable lids. Unlike most animals, the snake can neither open nor close its eyes. Instead, the snake has a transparent, hard shield covering each eye. This is important to the snake's way of life. With lids such as ours, it would never be able to crawl successfully through the brush, grass, and cactus in search of food. Closed eyes could see nothing, and when open the snake would constantly be in danger of something getting into them, impairing its sight.

A snake's eye shields become scratched and worn, and, about the time they begin to hamper vision, the snake is ready to shed its skin. Being part of the skin, the scratched outer shields are shed with the skin, leaving fresh, unmarred, shields in their place. In preparation for shedding, a liquid forms between the old and new shields to separate them. The snake's eyes become milky and its sight is reduced almost to the point of blindness. This condition lasts for several days, or until the separation is completed and the liquid dried up. During this partial blind period, the snake is rather irritable and is wary of enemies, so it usually coils up and remains in some safe area. A day or two later, the eyes clear, the snake sheds, and good vision is restored.

That Flicking Tongue

The tongue of a snake is often called a "stinger," even though it has been proved to be perfectly harmless. It is used by the snake as part of the sense of smell with which it locates prey, recognizes some enemies, and finds a mate.

The sense of smell is all-important to a snake, possibly more

A tongue flicking from the snake's closed mouth

important than its limited sense of sight. A snake does have functional nostrils, but it uses its tongue more than its nose for detecting odors. Any moving or alert snake may be seen to run its tongue in and out constantly. The mucus-coated forks at its tip are not sense organs, however, but merely tools to pick up scent and bring it back into the snake's mouth much as you or I would touch a substance and bring a finger to the nose for identification. In the roof of the mouth there are two openings that lead to glands called Jacobson's organs. These are the real olfactory organs and contain the nerves connected with the sense of smell. Each tip of the retracted tongue will slip into an opening just long enough for the glands to register whatever odor may be clinging to it. A small notch at the tip of the snake's nose permits the tongue to pass in and out when the mouth is almost closed.

It isn't necessary for the tips of the tongue to touch an object in order to establish identity. Most odors are transported through the air by water vapor or by tiny particles, and either can be collected readily by the tips and carried to the glands.

Any snake that, because of some accident, permanently loses the use of its tongue is quite apt to die. It would either be killed by an enemy which it was too slow in identifying or it might starve, being incapable of locating sufficient food.

The Amazing Heat Pits

It was not until the 1930s that the pit on each cheek of a rattlesnake was ascertained to be used for registering radiated heat. Prior to this, it was thought to have been a form of an ear, an additional nostril, or possibly a tactile organ that registered differences in air pressure. To discover and prove the true function of these pits, a series of experiments was conducted at The American Museum of Natural History in New York City.

The experiments were rough on the rattlesnakes, but did

On the same level but to the right of the snake's eye is the nostril, while in between and below is the heat pit.

clear up approximately 400 years of speculation. A snake was placed on top of a table that was covered with heavy sponge. This eliminated all vibrations that might be carried to the snake. The table legs were also set on sponge, and the experimenters were in their stocking feet and walked carefully. Next, opaque tape covered the eyes of the snake to prevent any vision, and waxed plugs were carefully inserted in the nostrils so that odor was blocked. This left the agile tongue, which the scientists snipped off. From all known facts, this snake was now completely cut off from its surroundings.

Using either covered electric light bulbs or balloons as targets —either of which could be heated or cooled readily—the experimenters tied them to long poles so that they could wave them close to the snake, yet not be close themselves where their own body temperature could affect the experiment. They found that cool bulbs or balloons produced no reaction unless the snake was touched. When the targets were heated and passed nearby, the snake would turn its head to follow the movement, or strike at it. When the warmth of the target radiated sufficient heat to raise the temperature next to the snake's heat pit as little as one-third of a degree, it alerted the snake. The distance from which the snake can detect an object warmer than the surrounding air is short, about 10 inches and not over 12.

These pits are located on either side of the rattlesnake's head, below and between the eye and nostril. They are called loreal, heat, or labial pits and are extremely sensitive. In the spring or during a hot, dry spell, when the grass is low and offers no concealment under which the snake can approach its food, it is often forced to go down gopher or prairie dog holes in search of prey. There may be many holes to examine before one is found that is occupied, and with its tongue and heat pits, the snake can often learn which is which from the surface of the ground. The rattler merely pokes its head down the hole, flicks its tongue to find out if there is fresh scent, and, if there is, it may probe deeper. If the animal is down the hole, the temperature of the hole will be a trifle warmer and will register on the snake's heat pits. If the hole is deserted, the pits will register cold and the rattler tries another hole.

Should both tongue and heat detectors register occupancy, the rattler crawls down in search of the animal. As the snake descends, it becomes too dark for even adjustable eyes to see anything. The tongue would guide it, but in the confinement of the burrow the odor of the creature would be clinging to the

38

Striking at small mammals hiding under such cactus plants often results in needles in the nose or side of the head.

sides of the tunnel and hang so heavy in the air that it would be confusing. Now the snake must depend entirely on its heat pits and it continues to crawl until they register considerable warmth. By swinging its head from side to side until an equal amount of heat registers in both pits, the snake knows that it is aiming directly at the animal. Because the pits register only at the proper striking distances, it strikes accurately.

During midsummer the surface of the prairie often becomes too hot for the cold-blooded rattler, so it hunts by night. Although the prey can be seen by the snake with its night vision, and followed by scent, it is the loreal pits with their heat sensitivity that guide the fangs accurately when the snake strikes. The pits are also used to determine in what area the snake should rest for either cooling itself down or for warming up. They are much more sensitive and register minute temperature changes faster than most man-made instruments can.

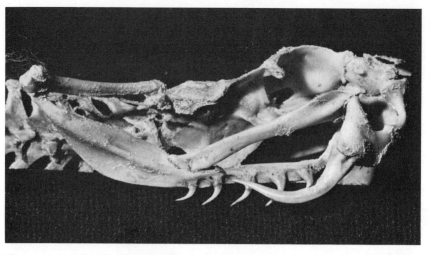

The actual skull of a diamondback rattler, showing the bones and arrangement of the upper jaw which holds teeth. The lower jaw is missing.

Mechanics of the Fangs

The fangs of the rattlesnake are its only armament, and the strike and withdrawal by a prairie rattlesnake are made with considerable speed, yet give the rattler ample time to inject its lethal venom. The arrangement and function of the fangs are ideal for this purpose. Fangs are long, hollow, curved teeth that are needle sharp at the tips. The venom is forced into an opening at the base of these teeth and issues from a slitlike opening near the tip. The fangs are not themselves movable, but are attached to a small maxillary bone which can rotate back and forth. This movement is necessary in vipers because the fangs are so proportionately long that unless they can be folded back parallel to the upper jaw when not in use, the snake could not shut its mouth without biting itself. When the fangs are erected for use, their tips protrude farther out than the snake's nose.

Occasionally when a rattler bites an animal, the creature jumps enough to cause one or both of the hollow, brittle fangs to be broken off. Depending as it does upon poison to kill its prey, the rattler would probably starve if it had no fangs with which to inject this venom. To avoid this possibility, the rattler gains two new fangs and sheds the old ones about every three weeks. The snake has what might be termed a fang factory at the back of each of its upper jaws. Here new fangs are constantly being produced and, as they grow, they move forward suddenly to appear in a socket waiting for them on the movable bone. This is possible because each of the maxillary bones has sockets for two fangs, although only one is normally present. Occasionally a rattlesnake is found in which the new fangs have moved in and the old ones have not yet been shed, thus making a four-fanged snake.

Both fangs and venom are present and functional at the instant of a rattler's birth. Often the fangs are too soft and small for much penetration of any hard surface, but the soft bodies of the small prey which a baby rattlesnake must eat, are easily punctured. At birth, a prairie rattler's fangs are less than a quarter of an inch long, but the adult snake may have fangs a full half-inch. Large snakes, such as the great diamondbacks, may acquire fangs over an inch or so long. Truly formidable weapons!

The opening for the release of the venom is not at the tip of the fang. Lest a tip opening be plugged with flesh or fur as it enters the prey, nature has placed the slit opening just above a solid tip, and on the front of the curve. A long slit on the front forms a much larger opening than a pin-sized hole at the end of the sharp point could possibly ever be, and, because the bite and injection of poison takes place in a fraction of a second, this larger opening is essential to releasing enough venom. The arrangement also lessens the possibility of breaking the point, as it must often pierce tough muscle, or it may even glance off a bone.

Due to the shorter length of a prairie rattler's fangs, and the

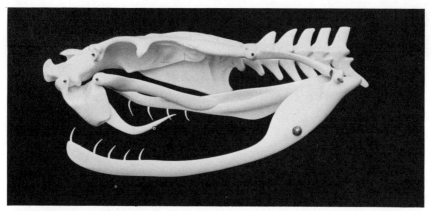

A model rattlesnake skull shows the function of the bones enabling the snake to open its mouth wide enough to encompass fairly large bodies of food, and close it in such a way that the fangs do not penetrate its lower jaws.

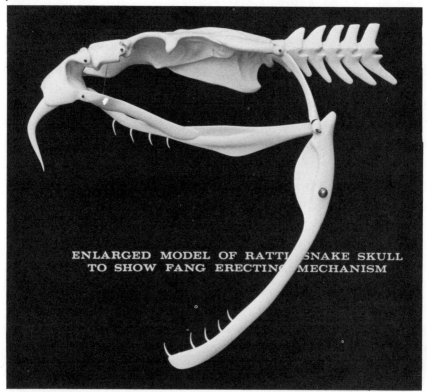

ENLARGED MODEL OF RATTLESNAKE SKULL
TO SHOW FANG ERECTING MECHANISM

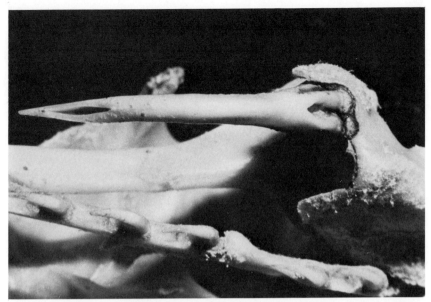

Two views of a diamondback's fang, showing curvature and openings. The fang is attached to the rotating maxillary bone.

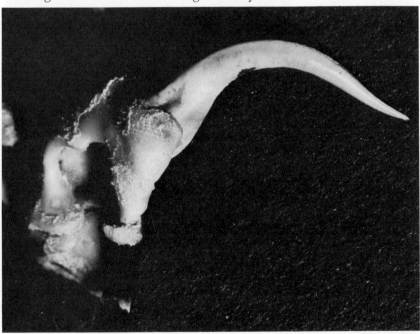

lighter weight of this snake, they seldom pass far enough through the leather of a good boot for an effective bite. The large diamondbacks, however, easily thrust their longer fangs through an average boot, the underlying socks, and well into a man's leg. People who consistently work with such snakes usually wear a special, high, tough, snakeproof boot, such as the Gokey. It is constructed of an extra thick, 8–9 ounce, specially tanned bull hide leather. They are 18 inches high and have consistently withstood the fangs of our largest rattlesnake. Any fairly high, reasonably new, good boot does help in rattlesnake country.

The Venom and Its Use

The poison of a rattlesnake is a modified saliva, produced in modified salivary glands called the parotids, and, like saliva, it is constantly being made. The glands that produce it are located on either side of the snake's head and are surrounded by muscles that control its use. At the extent of a rattler's strike, the muscles press down on the venom glands and force the poison through ducts that lead to the fangs. The snake has complete control of how much is forced out. It can squeeze hard and about empty the glands in one strike, or it can squeeze gently and dole out smaller amounts in a series of strikes.

Not too long ago it was believed that only three different types of venoms were found in the snakes of the world, so all the poisonous snakes were more or less classified into groups according to the type of poison they produced. Unable to break down and analyze venom, science originally had to analyze the victims. Cobra venom created nerve destruction and was called neurotoxic. The poison of an African snake named the boomslang caused considerable hemorrhage so was named a hemorrhagic snake, and the rattlesnake poison, which combines with and destroys blood, so earned the name haemotoxic. Modern chemis-

44

A tight, but gentle grip is needed when "milking" venom from a diamond-back.

try and physics have finally succeeded in breaking down and analyzing the venom itself and have proved the three divisions far too simple. Snake venoms are undoubtedly the most complicated poisons known. They are composed basically of numerous protein compounds, many of which are present in all venoms, but in different proportions. A predominance of the protein polypeptids in cobra venom are responsible for nerve destruction, and the greater number of enzymes in rattlesnake venom cause the blood and tissue destruction; yet some polypeptids exist in rattler venom, and enzymes are present in the cobra poison. Some cobra venom will destroy blood and tissue, and many of the rattlesnake species are almost as neurotoxic as are the cobras.

Poisonous snakes use their venom for two main purposes:

45

first, to immobilize and secure their prey and to start breaking down the tissues to be digested; and second, as a protection against enemies. All the rattlesnakes are poisonous but all of them do not have the same type of poison. Usually the venom of a rattler is sufficient in quantity and of enough strength to subdue an animal quickly of the size the rattler can readily swallow. The prairie rattler has such venom. A mouse or chipmunk dies rapidly, but a warm-blooded animal of a hundred or more pounds can often resist the venom's action and doesn't die, although it usually suffers much pain, discoloration, and swelling.

The larger eastern diamondback has a much more powerful venom, both in quality and in quantity. Its venom has more of the nerve-blocking qualities associated with cobra venom. In the Mohave Desert a medium-sized rattler, called appropriately the Mohave rattlesnake or *Crotalus scutulatus*, has a venom with almost pure nerve-blocking tendencies. It is a very dangerous snake because this venom works so fast; much faster than an equal amount of prairie rattler or diamondback poison. The

The Mohave rattlesnake, *Crotalus s. scutulatus*. The markings are bordered with white and fade out toward the tail. The dark bands encircling the tail are much narrower than the white.

This man milks a timber rattlesnake. Its venom will be frozen and sent to a laboratory.

rattlers of both Central and South America also have this fast-acting, message-blocking venom.

The poison of the prairie rattlesnake and of most of the rattlers of the United States is basically of the blood- and tissue-destroying type. This venom is high in what is called enzymatic action. It combines with and destroys the blood cells and breaks down muscle and other tissues. It slowly spreads its destruction throughout the victim, changing the body chemistry by hydrolysis. The poison continues its work until it is used up, removed by suction, or neutralized by a medicine known as antivenin.

Antivenin is made from the blood serum of an animal, such as a horse, goat, or rabbit, into whose blood stream the venom is injected in controlled doses. The venom induces antibody production in the animal's blood. Withdrawal and processing of small amounts of blood serum provides an antivenin for the bite of the species of rattler whose venom was used. New refinement allows some antivenins to be mixed, producing treatment for the bites of more than one species of rattler. However, even the new polyvalent antivenins have limitations and should be used only by professionals.

47

How the Rattler Moves

People have believed for years that snakes walked on their ribs because, when you look closely at the point of contact with the rattler's belly and the earth, there is a backward and forward motion to the belly plates. This, however, cannot be the only answer, because when a rattler wants to move fast, it does. Obviously, the limited movements of ribs could not propel it at too great a speed.

Some years ago, the herpetologist, Dr. James Oliver, assisted by photographer Samuel Dunton, took a viper to Rochester, New York, where the equipment was available, and, by a process called fluorography, made an X-ray film of a viper crawling and proved conclusively that the ribs remain perfectly still, yet the skin performed its back and forth movement. Further study showed that the ribs acted only as a support for the skin, much

The Great Basin rattler, *Crotalus v. lutosus*, is closely related to the prairie rattler, but has more vivid markings on a brownish background.

as the wheels of a tank support its endless tread. Small muscles attached to the skin lifted section after section of the belly skin, moved it forward, set it down, and pulled back. This action propels the rattler at a slow, sedate, or hunting pace.

To go faster, it uses its entire body to push against any projection that it may encounter. Each stone, plant, twig, tuft of grass, or hump in the ground is pressed upon by the sides of the snake as it moves forward. By undulating or waving the body, it can take advantage of so many points that the snake doesn't seem to be pushing on anything. Our eyes can hardly distinguish the fact that, with such contacts, it is actually tacking across the ground as a sailboat tacks across the wind.

All rattlesnakes use these two methods of movement, except the sidewinder which lifts the forepart of its body to one side, places it on the sand, and brings the rear half over. It looks awkward, forces the snake to travel sideways, and leaves a broken trail behind, but it is astonishingly fast and efficient.

The Rattle

The most unique part of a rattlesnake is the rattle. It is the one thing that separates it from all other types of snakes in the world. When a rattler is born, it comes into the world with what is called the prebutton on the end of its tail. Within a few days the baby sheds its skin for the first time, and, with this shed, the outer covering of the prebutton goes too, leaving the first true segment or button.

Moments after birth a disturbed prairie rattlesnake will vibrate its tail so fast that the button becomes a blur. There is no sound, however, because it is the clicking together of several segments of the rattle that produces the noise; but as the snake grows older and acquires several segments, it will make a sound that can be heard for 20 to 30 feet away. A large diamondback, with its huge rattle, can make an authoritative sound, not soon

The complete, unbroken rattle of a snake about two years old

Cross section of a broken rattle shows the convolutions of growth that anchor the new segments inside the old.

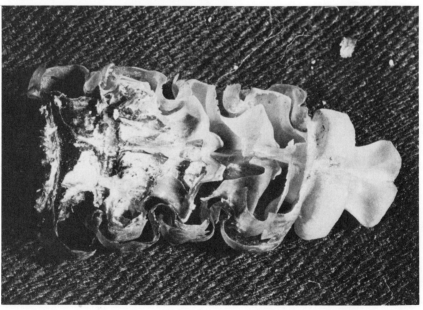

to be forgotten, whereas the tiny rattle of a pigmy rattler sounds more like the buzz of an insect.

The rattle is made up of a hardened or cornified skin, and each time the snake sheds, a new, slightly larger segment is deposited on the rattle at its junction with the snake. These are loosely joined together by being formed partly inside the older segments and are locked into place by the matching convolutions of them all. The length of the string or number of segments does not reflect the snake's age. A short, cool summer can reduce shedding to twice, with only two segments added, or the snake may gain four segments the following year if the weather is warm and food plentiful.

The prairie rattler does not always sound off. One may buzz when you approach within 20 feet, while others almost allow

A dangerous snake! This eastern diamondback has no rattle. With its rattle amputated behind the growing point, the snake can never make any warning sound.

you to step over them and never use their rattle. Science has long wondered why only this group of snakes in the entire world possess the rattle, or of what use it is to the snakes. Knowing that snakes are deaf, it's inconceivable that rattlers can know they are making any sound as they vibrate their tails. Equally confusing is the fact that many species of snakes that have no rattles vibrate their tails with equal vigor under similar circumstances. Possibly, like dogs that wag their tails to register happiness, snakes vibrate theirs to register nervousness. Rattles are often said to be warning devices. Unquestionably, the buzz will frighten away certain enemies, but, at the same time, the noise undoubtedly attracts some too.

Rainy days, heavy dew, or even thick fog will silence all the rattlers in the vicinity. Once water has penetrated the touching points of a rattle there will be no sound, although the snake continues to vibrate its tail as vigorously as ever.

CHAPTER 4

Obtaining Food and Water

In some ways, being cold-blooded actually aids the snakes because the lack of a body temperature greatly reduces the need for food. Where warm-blooded mammals seek food constantly, the rattlesnake often goes for several weeks or even months without any food at all. The warm-blooded or endothermic mammals require considerable fuel to create and maintain an internal temperature of 98.6 degrees or often higher. The rattlesnake needs food or fuel only for growth and minimal activity.

A sweating mammal needs a greater amount of water to replace the loss incurred by perspiration, whereas the waterproof rattler skin retains the body fluids. The snake also conserves water by having no liquid urine to dispose of. The rattler has no bladder for urine storage. Rather, when the feces nears the end of the intestinal tract, most of the water is reabsorbed by the body. The urea is eliminated as a paste of uric acid along with the semisolid feces. Such saving makes considerable difference on the great prairie. The rattler can easily coil up for days during inclement weather with no apparent suffering or deterioration and still eat sufficient food when the weather moderates to enable it to live for months.

Finding and catching its food are not as difficult for the rattle-

Cottontails, especially their young, are a favorite item of diet for prowling rattlesnakes.

snake as many people think. The small mammals and few birds that these snakes eat are plentiful on the prairie. Admittedly, these creatures are much faster than a slow-moving rattlesnake, and were the food creatures aware of the snake's potential they would certainly run, jump, or fly away with ease. But, for several reasons, the prey is seldom aware.

The prairie rattler, with its dry skin and without fur or feathers to absorb and retain odor, has little or no smell to advertise its presence. Its long, legless shape and sinuous motion enable it to glide across the prairie and through the grasses with little sound or warning vibrations. Furthermore, the hunted animals are seldom aware of the size of the snake. Being down on the ground themselves, they see only the snake's head and its flashing tongue as it glides silently and slowly through the grass. Invariably, the head of the snake is smaller than the food it hunts, and stimulates no fear. If anything, the little animals are more curious than frightened, and the snake has ample time to approach within striking range.

54

Sometimes the rattler resorts to ambush. Locating a fresh mouse trail by odor, it lies beside it until a mouse comes by then strikes it from behind a clump of grass. A snake will eat about anything of warm blood that it can swallow. Exceptions are occasionally made by the very young rattlers who do eat small lizards and the swamp rattler or massasauga that accepts a frog now and then.

A snake eats like no other creature in the world. Because it has no chewing teeth, the rattler must swallow its food as it finds it. It is unable to alter the size, shape, or in any way cut or tear it into smaller pieces, though the snake's venom does help by destroying tissue. When the prey is larger than the head of the snake which is about to engulf it, the rattlesnake must use its elastic jaws. Its lower jaws are not firmly attached to the skull; instead, the back of the lower jaws are loosely attached to the ends of movable bones called the quadrate. The other end of these quadrate bones is hinged to the skull. When the snake opens its mouth, the front of the lower jaw drops down, almost perpendicular to the upper jaw. By swinging or pivoting the quadrate bones from the skull, the rear of the lower jaws are also lowered, creating an enormous vertical expansion. In addition, the snake has no solid chin. The front ends of the lower jaw do not meet as a solid bone, but end abruptly and are joined by an elastic tissue. This enables the lower jaws to swing far apart or individually move back and forth. There are no muscles to drop the rear of the lower jaw or to spread the lower jaws apart. These movements are forced by the shape and size of the prey as it passes through.

The rattler usually selects the head end of its prey as a starting point for swallowing. The snake merely opens its mouth and starts to crawl around its food. A gopher or small prairie dog is much larger than the head of a prairie rattler and will take some time and effort. Often the snake will extend its fangs and, using

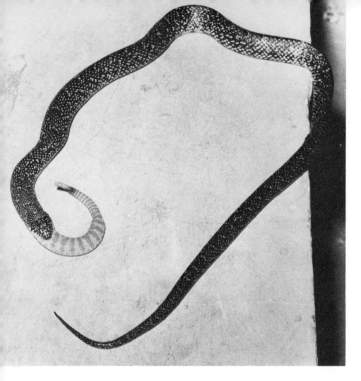

This speckled king snake, *Lampropeltis getulus splendida*, is swallowing an adult prairie rattler.

them as hooks, pull back on the food to aid in forcing it down the throat. Small food, like mice, will go down amazingly fast. Once past the mouth, the big struggle is over. The body muscles ahead of the lump will relax and the muscles behind will compress, squeezing the animal into the snake's stomach as we squeeze toothpaste from a tube.

All this would be impossible if the skin did not stretch. Some rattlesnakes swallow food so large that one would think the skin would burst and occasionally it does. After digestion begins, digestive gasses, if generated too fast, can exert enough pressure to split the snake wide open.

At best, a snake is uncomfortable after swallowing such a mass of food. With its stomach full, it is in no condition to fight enemies, nor does it care to travel. It usually finds a safe area and waits for digestion to reduce the bulge, taking several days. Such complete meals require considerable digestion and the snake's stomach fluids are adequate, being among the most powerful known. Hair, fur, feathers, scales, and bones are partially digested, and all of the softer tissues of the animals are reduced to their basic compounds. This method of eating also provides a great amount of the liquids that a snake needs. By swallowing a complete creature, all the fluids within that animal are absorbed by the snake.

There are times on the high prairie when a long dry spell evaporates much of the standing water of stock dams or natural ponds. Most prairie or desert mammals can dig down to cool depths and wait out the drought, obtaining their food and drink by nibbling on the deeper, moist roots of prairie or desert plants such as alfalfa and yucca, or by eating the moisture-loaded cactus pads. The snake, seeking food and shelter in these holes, obtains all its needs from the animals it swallows.

When rain reappears, the prairie rattler has been known to coil its body tightly so that the furrows between coils catch enough rainwater to allow the snake to suck it up.

As a result of eating too large an animal, this young Pacific rattler, *Crotalus v. oreganus*, has died from internal pressure. It is related to the prairie rattler, but is much darker in color. West Coast people often call it a timber rattler.

CHAPTER 5

Reproduction and Birth

All snakes produce eggs, but some species lay eggs (oviparous), while others retain the eggs in the body until they are ready to hatch (ovoviviparous), then give birth to living young. The rattlesnakes are all ovoviviparous. Prairie rattlesnakes of the high northern plains usually mate in the fall but, due to the short growing season, will not produce the young until the fall of the next year. Thus the female rattlers of this biome produce an average of about seven or eight young every other year. Rattlers of the south, where they enjoy a more temperate climate and a longer summer, produce young every year. The entire reproductive cycle is difficult to pin down because it has been discovered that many females can store live healthy male sperm for periods of at least two years.

Male and female rattlers look so much alike that only a herpetologist can accurately tell them apart. The female organs, consisting of ovaries and the accessible canal leading to the cloaca, are all within the body and produce a slightly heavier looking snake. The male rattler, like all male snakes, has a reproductive organ known as a hemipenis. This is a bilobed organ consisting of two functional penises which are inverted, or tucked inside out, into the base of the snake's tail, and lies parallel to the body from the cloaca toward the rattle. Neither penis is used for urination, as snakes lack a bladder, but when used in reproduction, they are turned right side out, which forces them to extend from the cloacal opening.

In the fall the rattlers are attracted to each other by odor. After a preliminary courtship by the male, who pursues and rubs the female all over with several dilated tubercles on his chin, they mate. (These tubercles are apparent only during mating procedures.) Crawling alongside his mate, the male entwines the last few inches of his body around hers. She responds by curling her tail to meet his. The male penetrates her cloaca with the penis nearest her underside and it is locked into place by dilation of several fleshy spines on the skin of the penis. They stay locked together until the spines are deflated, sometimes for

A newborn prairie rattler showing its button.

as long as twelve hours. After separation, each snake goes its own way, presumably never to meet again.

The following fall the eggs within the female's body have produced the tiny rattlers, each enclosed in a transparent, cellophanelike bag called the amniotic sac. Often the young escape from these sacs while still within the mother's birth canal, but normally a convulsive movement of her body forces them out onto the ground, still containing the young. The mother has served her purpose and goes about her own business, but each little snake begins to revolve and probe, searching for a way out of its prison. Upon the tip of each young snake's nose there is an extremely small projection called the egg tooth, which aids in slitting the side of the amnion and allowing it to escape.

Snake young issue from the sacs in complete control of the situation. They all have functional fangs, full venom glands, a disposition which is normally nastier than that of their parents, and one segment of the rattle on the end of their tail. Within an average of ten days, each newborn sheds its skin for the first time. With this shed goes the little egg tooth and the outer covering of the prebutton. The young rattler now, except for its size, resembles the adult.

The same reproductive pattern applies to all rattlers, with the exception of the size and the number of young per litter. The larger species tend to have larger and more young.

CHAPTER 6

Enemies of the Rattler

It is inevitable that any creatures of moderate size have enemies, and the rattlesnakes are no exception. Some of them are hunted for food and others are destroyed merely to end the threat of being bitten.

On the great prairie it is the birds of prey which take the highest toll. The red-shouldered hawk, the eagle, and the short-eared owl, which hunts both day and night, can readily see and swoop down on the rattler that enjoys sparse cover for its activities. The sudden attack by powerful beaks and claws gives the snake little chance, and occasionally one or another of these birds are seen carrying a dangling snake as it flies away.

Another bird, the wild turkey, also kills rattlers when they are found in their feeding areas among the oak groves bordering parts of the prairie.

Badgers are reknown for being rattlesnake killers, destroying all they find. Some snakes are killed for food, but most seemingly out of pure cussedness, because these prairie animals will go to great lengths to find and destroy any and all snakes of any species. They have been known to tear apart a rancher's snake trap and strew the area with parts of any snakes it may have contained.

The short-eared owl is one of the enemies of the rattlesnake.

Red-shouldered hawks are not loath to dine on rattlesnakes.

Deer, both mule and white-tailed, range much of the prairie and its surrounding forests and often will stop to tread upon a prairie rattlesnake.

Deer and antelope have been seen pouncing on rattlesnakes with stiff front legs and sharp hooves, literally cutting them to pieces. Not meat-eaters, it is assumed both animals kill rattlers as a protective measure.

One of the least likely enemies of the prairie rattler is the prairie dog, yet they have been seen filling their own holes in an effort to trap, suffocate, and bury a rattler which they have seen crawl down one.

King snakes are cannibalistic, powerful constrictors, and almost totally immune to the poisons of rattlesnakes. They apparently do not hunt rattlers for food, but neither do they pass them by. I have seen a 34-inch, speckled king snake (*Lampropeltis splendida*) capture, partially suffocate by constriction, and finally swallow a prairie rattlesnake 2 inches longer than the cannibal king. A remarkable feat!

Desert rattlesnakes, usually the young, frequently are captured and eaten by the desert's most remarkable bird, the

63

roadrunner, whose speed and dexterity easily confuse and over-whelm the snake.

Domestic pigs consider the rattler excellent eating and with ease, they bite, chew, and stomp their way through the snake's defenses. Their wild cousins, the peccaries of the Southwest, use similar tactics with similar results.

Alligators in the Southeast seldom miss a chance to seize and eat a swimming or careless snake that approaches too close. A like fate befalls South American rattlers from the caiman, a cousin of the alligator.

All rattlers are subject to attacks from a tiny external parasite called the snake mite. Under the proper conditions these develop rapidly and can gradually suck the life from their host. Sometimes rattlers will shed prematurely in an effort to lose the mites with the lost skin, but mite eggs are tucked deep down in the nostrils and heat pits and often survive to carry on the attack.

In addition to the enemies mentioned, there are the occa-

The western milk snake, *Lampropeltis triangulum gentilis,* is one of the cannibalistic king snakes that prey on small prairie rattlers.

In a pinch, a wildcat or bobcat dares to attack the rattler
for food.

sional enemies, those which would rather give the rattlesnake a
wide berth, but due to poor hunting and a vigorous appetite,
will risk all for a meal. These include the fox, coyote, bobcat,
weasel, mink, otter, and several species of birds. Some natural-
ists have claimed to have seen large frogs and tiger salamanders
grasp and swallow newborn rattlers of different species.

South and Central American rattlesnakes undoubtedly have
more enemies than our northern species. Hordes of army ants,
against which there is no defense other than flight, must account
for some slow-moving reptiles. Large carnivorous toads and
frogs such as the horned or barking frog, Blombergs, and the
marine toad easily snap up and swallow young rattlesnakes.
Giant bird-eating spiders occasionally trap a small rattler in the
strong webbing and have a feast. A greater number of meat-
eaters such as the ocelot, jaguar, and other cats account for others. Also, South America has more ophiophagous or cannibalistic varieties of snakes to which a rattler is merely another meal.

The rattlesnakes have survived these enemies for thousands of
years, but all the natural enemies combined cannot equal the

65

Bison, due to their size, can withstand a snake's bite but, for the same reason, can easily squash a rattler by stepping on one.

latest and greatest threat to their existence, man.

Man has been the consistent enemy of snakes since the beginning of his recorded history and undoubtedly for his entire existence. Originally killing snakes for food, he probably killed also for self-preservation after discovering the poisonous potential of some types. Today, despite advanced knowledge concerning species and potential, the snake still finds few friends among humans. Indeed, so many people abhor and fear them that the term "ophidiaphobia" was coined expressing this feeling.

The spread of civilization and construction of its cities, towns, farms, and highways inadvertently killed great numbers of rattlers, but man still persists in the destruction. Protective wildlife laws are often declared to be not relevant where rattlesnakes are concerned, and it is difficult to refute the arguments of a man who has either been bitten himself, or has had farm stock, pets, or a child injured by a bite. Thus the hunting and killing of rattlers are regarded as protective measures by those who live among or near them. Not only are the individual snakes destroyed but located dens are dynamited, gassed, or covered.

National parks often take measures to protect the snakes, for they are important in maintaining the balance of nature. But even here, rattlers usually are moved from areas of heavy tourist traffic to areas less frequented by people. Often they are destroyed.

It has been shown that rodents increase as snake populations go down. Yet a great number of people still prefer to kill the snakes, and then control the rodents themselves by other means. Only in wilderness areas are the much maligned rattlers left alone.

It does seem inevitable that some species of rattlesnakes will eventually be exterminated, for civilization still spreads, and whenever it encompasses an entire biome, the indigenous wildlife is doomed.

CHAPTER 7
Spending the Winter

It is essential to rattlesnakes, especially those that live in the higher and more northern portions of their world, that they have ready access to rocky and fractured ledges. In these biomes the frost penetrates deep into the ground, and the ectothermic snakes would surely die if exposed to below-freezing temperatures for a prolonged time. The cracks in these rocks allow the snakes to go as deep as necessary, and in the high prairie the frost can go down 6 to 8 feet. Some rattlers do find deserted prairie dog holes that are deep enough for successful hibernation, but since the large dog towns have been destroyed, the snakes depend almost entirely on the rocky buttes and foothills.

Hibernating snakes slow down all the processes of life to a point approaching death. Such a condition requires little nourishment or moisture. During the summer months snakes store up enough fat to enable them to go without food or drink for almost a year. They also have the ability to produce, or synthesize, some of their own water as the stored fats are chemically altered into the necessary foods for maintaining this thin thread of life.

Snake dens can contain great numbers of rattlers. In a Wyoming barrel trap, emptied only once, over 150 prairie rattlesnakes

When winter comes to the plains, the deer march over the snow-covered dens of the hibernating snakes.

were captured. How many had managed to get out before the trap was set, or how many left the hole after the trap was removed, no one will ever know.

Rattlers that live at lower elevations where there is less frost need go underground for only 4 to 6 feet, and in the south where the climate is seldom or never freezing the snakes merely coil up under a log, in a stump, or under a pile of brush and wait out the cold spell. Rattlers of Central and South America never hibernate, and where hibernation is unnecessary, the snakes are less inclined to group or den.

As soon as the nights start to grow cold, the snakes of the northern regions return to their dens. Somehow, they must

An actual group of hibernating rattlesnakes, interspersed with an occasional blue racer, in a man-made den at the Black Hills Reptile Gardens.

know they will have to because they rarely travel for more than three miles from this point. The older snakes seem to know the way back and the newborn, which have never been there, must follow the scent trails of their elders. Sometimes, snakes will find an adequate rupture in the earth's surface located some distance from the original den and here they will remain over winter, returning again the following fall, and in this way distributing the species.

For several days, or even weeks if the daytime weather remains sufficiently warm, the snakes will cluster about the rocks or ledges that surround the dens. They sun themselves on warm days but retreat underground as the evening approaches. Fewer

70

of the snakes return to the surface each day until the last of them succumbs to the weather and crawls down into the dark, cool, but safe winter haven. Here they separate into groups of tightly enmeshed bodies, pressing up against each other for whatever warmth they can share.

Spring brings a reversal of the same procedure. As some of the warm spring air seeps down the crevice, it hastens the blood flow, awakens the snakes, and slowly entices them to the surface. The first few to come out merely lie in the sun for the warm part of the day and return to the den at night. Gradually, as both air and soil warm up, the snakes begin their annual three-mile trek in search of food. It is during the spring exodus that the farmers and ranchers set their snake traps at the entrances to known dens.

CHAPTER 8

Precautions When in Rattler Territory

Encountering a rattlesnake will probably be an unwelcome surprise for both snake and man, but it will have to be the thinking man who dominates the situation. The snake will probably strike if you are close enough, so high boots are recommended. New leather will defy all fangs but those of the large rattlers; and the sloppy rubber boot, although penetrated by the fang, seldom allows it to reach past the empty space between the boot and your leg.

Keep your hands high when walking through weeds and grasses that may be hiding a snake and never reach down when you can't see the ground. Over 90 percent of the bites take place on the lower arms and hand, or on the lower legs and feet. Some people carry a long stick and swish it over the grasses and weeds in hopes of forcing the snake to rattle. If it becomes necessary to lift a log or stone, lift it toward yourself so that any snake that may be under it will find the log or stone a barrier between your feet and its strike. When climbing slopes or cliffs, check the next hand grip carefully before reaching up. Ledges are favorite sunning places for many rattlers. Walk at a reasonable pace so

72

The prairie rattlesnake at home

that you see where you step. Walk with firm footsteps. The vibration in the ground warns the snake of your approach and often he will rattle, back off, or even leave. A surprised snake frequently strikes.

If you live in such an area or intend to be in one for any length of time, it would be a good idea to seek a little knowledge of the types of snakes to be found in this area from a recognized authority, such as your local zoo or college; then learn the accepted method of first aid for snakebite and the address and location of the nearest hospital where you can obtain antivenin. Because of the expiration dates and the infrequent calls for it, drug stores often do not stock it.

The timber rattlesnake, *Crotalus h. horridus*

One final precaution. Do not run from a rattlesnake. Because of their habits, there is always a good chance that where there is one, there can be others. Running in fear could conceivably lead you to another snake, but you would be moving too fast to stop. When you meet one, just stop, back up a step or two—slowly. Turn around and, with eyes and ears on the alert, try to walk out of the area on the same path you used coming in. The snake will not chase you!

CHAPTER 9

Rattlesnake Myths

There are no other creatures in the world that have generated as many erroneous beliefs as the snakes have, and due to their size, potential, and rattles, the rattlesnake is close to the top of the list. Some of these beliefs are:

The age of a rattler can be determined by counting the segments of the rattle.
All rattlesnakes are blind in August.
Rattlers always rattle before they strike.
A snake will not die before sundown.
Rattlers will not cross a horsehair rope.
A pistol pointed at a rattler never misses; the snake aims its head.
Snakes charm their prey.
Rattlers live in harmony with the burrowing owl.
Snakes swallow their young to protect them.
Exhibited rattlers are usually "fixed" or drugged so that they are safe to handle.
Fangs, remaining in the boot of a man bitten and killed, can also kill the son who wears the same boots years later.

There is one set of myths associated with the treatment of snakebites which are dangerous for the victim to believe in.

A freshly killed, split chicken applied to a snakebite sucks out the venom.

Whiskey is a good remedy.

Burning gunpowder applied to a bite burns out the poison.

Soaking in coal oil, potassium permanganate, hot, or near-freezing water is a good treatment for snakebite.

The best treatment is to see a doctor as soon as possible. Hundreds of man-hours over hundreds of years have gone into separating the myths from the facts that relate to the rattlesnakes. Many questions have been solved by simple observation, but those dealing with the venom and its action on people are too complicated for any simple answers. It has only been within the past few years that the analysis of venom has led to important discoveries relating to the proper care for elimination of suffering and the saving of life. It will probably take many more years to thoroughly understand and apply all the findings, and more years yet to live down the myths which are such a deep part of our folklore.

Perhaps we shall never know the whole story. As civilization moves in, the snakes, through necessity, move out. Even during my own lifetime, it has been necessary to branch out farther and farther to find fewer snakes. Maybe someday they will all be gone and we won't need to know; the rattlesnake itself will have become a myth.

Bibliography

Conant, Roger. 1958. *Field Guide to Reptiles & Amphibians.* Boston: Houghton.

Klauber, Laurence M. 1973. *Rattlesnakes: Their Habits, Life Histories & Influence on Mankind.* 2nd ed. 2 vols. Berkeley: Univ. of California Press.

Matthews, William H., III. 1962. *Fossils: An Introduction to Prehistoric Life.* New York: Barnes & Noble.

Oldham, Jonathan Clark. Laboratory Manual of Snake Anatomy. Thesis. Black Hills State College, Spearfish, South Dakota.

Romer, Alfred S. 1941. *Man & the Vertebrates.* 3rd ed. Chicago: Univ. of Chicago Press.

Schmidt, Karl P. and D. Dwight Davis. 1941. *Field Book of Snakes of United States and Canada.* New York: Putnam.

Index

About the Author

G. Earl Chace, who began his long experience with reptiles as keeper of snakes at the Bronx Zoo in New York City, lives in Rapid City, South Dakota, where he has been Curator of the Black Hills Reptile Gardens for over twenty years.

Mr. Chace is now Curator Emeritus and an instructor on poisonous reptiles, arachnids, and insects for the Emergency Medical Training Courses of the South Dakota State Department of Health. The author of numerous magazine articles and a weekly nature column, he also lectures in schools and is a member of the South Dakota area Endangered Species Committee for Amphibians and Reptiles. He is married and has a grown son and daughter.